Can You
See Them Now?

(Elephants in Our Midst!)

Discover the Hidden Elephants Lurking
in Your Organization or Work-Team...
Then Vanquish Them!

D1213798

CLAIR

ILLUSTRATED BY: CHRISTINE J. STOELTING

Can You See Them Now?
(Elephants in our Midst!)
Discover the Hidden Elephants Lurking in Your Organization or Work-Team…Then Vanquish Them!

Authored by: Claire Knowles
Illustrated by: Christine J. Stoelting

Claire E. F. Knowles
6083 Bahia del Mar Circle, # 564
St. Petersburg, FL 33715
1-716-622-7753
Claire@ClaireEKnowles.com
Claire@LightsOnLeadershipSuccess4Women.com
CEFK1@aol.com
www.CanYouSeeThemNow.com
www.LightsOnLeadershipSuccess4Women.com
www.LightsOnBook.com
www.ClaireEKnowles.com

Limits of Liability and Disclaimer of Warranty

The author and publisher shall not be liable for your misuse of this material. This book is strictly for informational and educational purposes.

Warning – Disclaimer

The purpose of this book is to educate and entertain. The author and/or publisher do not guarantee that anyone following these techniques, suggestions, tips, ideas, or strategies will become successful. The author and/or publisher shall have neither liability nor responsibility to anyone with respect to any loss or damage caused, or alleged to be caused, directly or indirectly, by the information contained in this book.

ISBN 10: 0972120467
ISBN 13: 978-09721204-6-3

What Is This Book About?

This book is about elephants. Organizational elephants. Elephants that hide in organizations and work-teams and prevent you, as a leader, and your organization or work-group from collectively being the best that you can be.

Ultimately, the success of businesses, organizations, teams, and work-groups depends on the quality of the people involved and their ability to interact effectively. And while resolving people- and non-people-related issues and conflicts (our organizational elephants) is not easy, it is not impossible either.

This book is about understanding elephants—about finding the hidden elephants. And once found, it is about garnering what's necessary to lift them up, seeing them from important and varied perspectives, and then addressing them—even vanquishing them for the long-term. And that is *not* easy.

If it were easy to do, then there would be no hidden elephants to find. If it were easy to do, then we would not all be able to immediately recognize phrases like these:

"There's a big, stinking elephant in the room."
"There's an elephant hiding under the rug."

And people would not shake their heads as if there was nothing that could be done when elephants take up residence under the rug, or, heaven forbid, if they begin to languish there and begin to stink.

So, besides being about hidden elephants, this book is, more importantly, about leaders, leadership, and responsibly finding and dissecting your organizational elephants. Why? So that your business, your organization, your work-team, your work-group can *thrive*!

Do you have to be a special leader to find organizational elephants? Absolutely not. Anyone can help lift up the elephants hiding and lurking in your workplace, team, group, or organization. This book will show you how to lift them up (from under the rug) and move forward effectively.

Acknowledgements/Dedication

Acknowledgements:

I extend a special "thank you" to all who have encouraged me to complete this business book-writing project about lifting up our elephants. Particularly, I acknowledge this one impetus: While facilitating an evening business networking event, I asked everyone around the table whether anyone had any "elephants" hiding in their organizations. Everyone at the table chuckled at first, but then, slowly, each began to share glimpses of their respective elephants. *Having listened carefully to these women and men talk uncomfortably about their elephants and be noticeably unsure of what could be done about them*, I knew this book needed to be written.

While everyone knows there are elephants lurking, few can or will diligently go forward to find them—to address and resolve them for the long-term. That's why phrases like *elephant in the room* and *elephant under the rug* live on. Thus, I'm compelled to lift them up with language to which all can relate. Can you see them now? (In elephant-speak!)

Thanks also to my women's network colleagues for your solid and continuous support of my work: Business Professional Women (BPW), The YWCA, WesternNewYorkWomen.com, St. Petersburg Chamber Women's Leadership Council's INSPIRE leaders, New York State Women Inc., Zonta International, the Interfaith Council, NAWBO, ABWA, and Women Leaders everywhere!

Dedication:

This book is lovingly dedicated to my husband, Richard, and to my daughter, Christine, who has generously provided the illustrations herein.

It is also dedicated to Beth, Dorothy, and Cynthia, three wonderful women who, as my stepdaughters, continue to enrich my life.

Claire Knowles

About the Author

Best-selling author **Claire Knowles** is an experienced, knowledge-able Human Resources Management and Labor Relations professional. She approaches her work from the perspective of a deep belief in the goodness of people.

Her openness, honesty, and sense of fairness, combined with her instincts for what it takes to find the higher ground, has made her one of the most effective people in this field. She retired from the DuPont Company, where her professional career spanned 33 years and encompassed the breadth of Human Resource Management and Labor Relations.

She has since transitioned to the role of Independent Leadership Consultant and Coach. She is also a full partner in R. N. Knowles & Associates, Inc. She currently assists leaders, organizations, and teams collaboratively find clear paths of action to complete their work and achieve personal goals, fully aligned with clear principles. She is a people person, a deep listener, and she uses the Living Systems approach to problem solving for personal and organizational change efforts.

Claire graduated from the State University of New York with a degree in Business Management and Economics. She majored in Human Resource Management and Labor Relations. In addition, she is certified in Mediation, a course recognized by the N.Y. State

Unified Court System. She is also an OSHA-certified safety training professional.

Claire is the Amazon best-selling author of *Lights On! A Reflective Journey...Illuminations to Move Your Life Forward with Ease* ©2012 and the creator of Lights On! Workshop©—especially for women.

Claire's work is with leaders, organizations, teams, and work-groups (women and men), including Success Workshops, Speaking Engagements, Consulting, Facilitation, Presentations, Retreats, Coaching, and, particularly, helping women's organizations and women-run businesses *become the very best they can be (together)*.

About the Illustrator

Illustrator Christine J. Stoelting lives in Buffalo, N.Y. and is a product management and brand strategy professional working within the food and beverage industries. She holds both an MBA and a Master of Science in Marketing from the Simon Graduate School of Business, as well as a BA in French, Spanish, and International Relations from the University of Rochester.

Since her childhood, Christine has enjoyed writing, drawing, and channeling her inner-creative in her free time and in her work. She is happy and proud to provide the illustrative content for this book, and to work closely on this creative and important project alongside her mother, Claire.

Christine is also the creator and developer of the *Color Me Perfect* iPhone app, which synthesizes her unique humor with numerological algorithms and daily color choices to help her app users make the perfect color choice for their outfit each day.

Foreword

by Richard N. Knowles
Author of *The Leadership Dance*
...Pathways to Extraordinary Organizational Effectiveness

Effective leaders are able to sense what is happening in their organizations and make adjustments to the leadership processes they use as circumstances and conditions change. The Leadership Dance is the ability to move among Self-Organizing Leadership, Operational Leadership, and Strategic Leadership so that they (leaders and their teams) are in tune with their complex, changing environment.

But many organizations have serious burdens that hamper their ability to be nimble, quick, and fully aware of their circumstances. Many organizations share that they are trying to move quickly, but can't take the time that they should to see and understand what is happening in their environment and find what is blocking their progress and slowly eroding their success. (That is an elephant!)

In my many years of leading industrial organizations and now in my own consulting business, I see how the failure of leaders to hunt their elephants, find them, address them, reflect on them, and ensure they don't come back is often totally missed. When Claire Knowles first shared that this was the book subject she most wanted to lift up for leaders—I heartily encouraged her to do so. Her highly successful work with leaders and their organizations in consulting and in doing organizational assessments and change management is a prime example of how to lift up elephants.

Organizations behave as if they are complex living systems; within that organizational complexity is where the elephants hide. It truly is hard to describe an elephant. Those non-descriptions become clues to the hidden elephants that prevent the free flow of ideas and information, the development of trusting and interdependent relationships, and the ability of people to see and connect with the whole system. Finding, naming, and addressing these elephants are the keys to building a winning organization.

Where do the elephants come from?

Where do they hide?

Can we afford to keep and feed them while our organization stagnates, languishes, and dies?

Can we address and resolve or send these elephants back (to the jungle) from which they came and restore our vitality and health, becoming nimble, quick, and more competitive?

This important book provides a light-hearted approach to a very serious business issue that may be costing your organization its future. Claire Knowles brings you insights and stories that will help you find and address your elephants. She'll help you see the cost of keeping and feeding them. And when you've named them, just see how quickly they can then be openly addressed. There are important processes that leaders can learn to use to effectively address their elephants.

> Elephants come from many places.
> Elephants are good at hiding.
> Elephants are very expensive.
> Elephants can be found and addressed.

The author also shows you how to open up the free flow of information and create the organizational safety for people to talk about them. Then off they go! Watch them run!

You will appreciate the way deeper threads of leadership are wonderfully woven throughout the chapters—each presenting important lessons for leaders.

Richard N. Knowles, Ph.D.

For the Reader

The major chapters of this book are each divided into four related segments.

1. The chapter title and corresponding elephant illustration.
2. The perspective in *elephant-speak.*
3. The perspective in *business-speak.*
4. A whimsical, yet thought-provoking summary.

The final three chapters deviate somewhat from this pattern because of the numerous examples provided.

This book is purposely written this way. Being in the position of the ignored elephant in the room or of the elephant hiding under the rug are important perspectives to understand. You'll see how these significantly connect when standing in the place of the business leader.

Lastly, note that elephants in the room or under the rug don't have to be there, stay there, or return there. Leaders who understand how to find them, lift them up, and address them can do that—if they want to—and if they are willing to step up to create the elephant-free environment that so many people in organizations, businesses, teams, and work-groups are craving. We all want to *thrive!* And you can be that special elephant-vanquishing leader!

Here's to you and your organization!

Contents

Introduction:
Speaking of Organizational Elephants

- Elephants hide in organizations, teams, and work-groups.

- Elephants hide under the rug and in meeting rooms.

- Elephants are difficult to see, to find, and to describe.

- Elephants are everywhere. They are pervasive. And overall, elephants do not like change. They prefer the status quo.

- Elephants are generally negative, yet there are a few positive ones.

- Negative elephants hinder organizations, teams, and work-groups from being the best they can be together.

- Elephants that are lurking and not found and addressed begin to stink. Sometimes they fester.

- Elephants that are not addressed will multiply and beget more elephants.

- One elephant can transform into several elephants.

- Elephants wonder if they'll ever be found, named, and addressed.

- Elephants wonder why making them visible is so difficult.

- Elephants wonder why people ignore them.

- Elephants wonder why people are afraid to name them.

- Elephants wonder why people hesitate to lift up the rug and look for them there.

- Elephants love to have courageous leaders discover them.

- Elephants love to have authentic leaders address them. Integrity matters!

- Elephants know there are processes that effective leaders can use to address them.

- Once elephants have been found and addressed, if the organization is *not* alert and cautious, new elephants can come and take up residence under the very same rug!

- Elephants believe that they, the elephants, are *not* the problem; rather, they believe that people who are unwilling to find them are the real concern.

- Elephants know that once people discover the secret to finding them, lifting them up, naming them, and addressing them, that *life in the organization, team, or work-group is so much better and hugely more effective.*

Chapter 1:
There's an Elephant Hiding Out Here!

Elephant-speak:

> Elephants like to play games. We like to *hide out*.
> Often we are in a room…in a Staff Meeting, in a
> Boardroom, or in a Team Meeting or Group Meeting.
>
> Oh, we are there, all right! The game we play is that
> most of the time we are invisible! Sometimes we
> like to hide out…under the rug!
>
> There are some very smart people who have a
> special sense of perception. They can smell an elephant!
> They know that an elephant is in the room…somewhere!
> They just can't see it! Or, if they're lucky enough to
> happen to have a special sight-sensory gift, they might be
> able to peek at the elephant and see just a brief glimpse,
> but they may not be brave enough to talk about it.
>
> If they only knew the *secret* to making elephants
> fully visible! Then everyone could see the same elephant.
> Then everyone could talk about it…together!

Business-speak:

The well-known expression, *elephant in the room,* is an English idiom for an obvious truth that is being ignored, avoided, or is going unaddressed, usually for a considerable amount of time. The expression also applies to a problem, situation, or risk that no one wants to discuss. Thus, in the business world, we call these elephants that we don't or won't talk about *"un-discussables."*

Logically, you would think that an elephant in a room would be impossible to overlook, avoid, or ignore! They are so big, right? So extending this *elephant in the room* metaphor means that people in the room who have a sense that it is there but ignore it, or avoid it, or pretend the elephant is not there, have actually made a choice. They are choosing to concern themselves with other things, perhaps smaller and/or irrelevant issues rather than dealing with the looming big one—the one that's lurking right in front of them—the one they don't/won't/can't acknowledge as there.

TuSK...TuSK...TuSK:

An Elephant is in here?
In this room?
Are you sure?
Where? Where is there an elephant?
How do you know that?
I don't see anything here.

Chapter 2:
Elephants Can Get Really Stinky!

Elephant-speak:

Sometimes the *elephant in the room* is referred to as the stinky elephant, the dead elephant, the sleeping elephant, or the elephant hiding under the rug.

Sometimes elephants hiding under the rug actually can get so old that we die under there…and leave a big lump! Still, people seem to be oblivious, and walk right around these lumps in the rug! Sometimes they are afraid to look under the rug to see what's really there.

It matters not what elephants are labeled…it can be stinky, dead, sleeping, or hiding under the rug. We all know what the presence of an elephant means: Trouble for you! Trouble for your organization or work-team.

Big trouble!

Business-speak:

There are elephants in the boardroom and in the back room. They are hiding in organizations—nonprofits, for-profits, partnerships, municipalities, and academia. They hide at the board level, staff level, and team level. They are in department head meetings and lunchrooms. They are in offices and on the factory floor. They're spoken of in hushed tones around the water cooler, in the break room, and in the ladies' room and men's room.

An *undiscussable* is just that—something that is allowed to go *undiscussed*—at least publicly. Make no mistake, however, what goes unsaid in front of the hierarchy does get whispered about in other places. It goes underground. This negatively affects the health and maturity of an organization, business, team, or work-group, and ultimately, it impacts the organization's success. It impacts the collective effectiveness of the entity as a whole.

TuSK…TuSK…TuSK:

What's Your Elephant's Name?
It's hiding in the Boardroom, the Back Room,
the Break Room, and the Bathroom!

You haven't noticed? Are you Sure?
Have you looked under the rug?

Chapter 3:
Elephants Can Get So Stinky They Begin to Fester!

C. Stoelting

Elephant-speak:

Have you smelled the elephant in the room? How long have you been smelling it? What do you think happens when an elephant takes up residence in your workplace? We elephants can live for a long, long time. No place to take a bath! No one addressing us. So, guess what? We just keep getting smellier and smellier. Oh, my!

Interesting, isn't it, that the answers to how to expose us are already in the room, right along with us elephants? Festering doesn't have to happen. Each elephant can be uncovered and addressed, if you want it to be.

Leaders are in the best position to lift up elephants. Leaders are in the best position to create an environment where elephant identification is a safe activity in which others can engage.

Did you know that leaders can actually be one of the elephants— to whom no one is willing to say what they really think? Leaders can, conversely, be an effective elephant-lifting magnet. Leaders get to determine how many elephants are going to be taking up residence within their own organization or team.

Worth noting: you don't have to be a designated leader to see, smell, recognize, or lift up elephants! It's just that it takes a whole lot of gumption and grit to lift up that rug…and expose one of us elephants all by yourself!

Business-speak:

As a leader, you get what you ask for; you also get what you tolerate; and you also get what behaviors you model. Authenticity—especially when it comes to dealing with hidden elephants—is not something you have, it is something you choose. Do you want your organization's or work-team's elephants to be lifted up? Do you want transparency? Are you open to having them lifted up? How do you model that? Are you receptive or vindictive to those who would garner the courage to bring something forward? Is it safe for people to lift up elephants, or not? How do you know?

Recognizing that there is an *elephant in the room* is an acknowledgment that the issue is there and it is big—it is not going to go away by itself. Ask for help, and you'll be surprised about the additional resources that will step forward to help lift it up and address it. Living in an atmosphere of hiding elephants is not healthy for anyone, or for the business environment.

> **"Smart leaders and managers can smell and tell when there's a dusty, big, fat, hairy, smelly, messin'-n-stinkin' pachyderm in the workplace or house."**
> **~ Dr. Dennis O'Grady**

We are all leaders at some time…either through one's own volition, or by appointment, or by default. What differentiates good leaders is their effectivness. The best leaders *listen* to their followers and *inspire* them to move forward. Listening is an elephant-lifting skill. Inspiring groups to address the elephants keeping them from being the best they can be is a leadership skill!

TuSK...TuSK...TuSK:

An elephant is in the room.
It is being covered with perfume.
But now's the time to find it once and for all,
Now's the time for you to heed the call.

Chapter 4:
Introducing Hiney, the Hidden Elephant

Elephant-speak:

This is Hiney, the elephant. The *H* stands for hidden. Hiney is always hidden. He is one of the elephants that hides out in meeting rooms.

He never has his name revealed because no one will speak of him in front of the hierarchy, or even in one-to-one meetings with the hierarchy.

Yet, to stay alive, he must be fed. Hmmm. What could it be that is feeding Hiney?

Business-speak:

Many cultures have a word for *undiscussables,* a.k.a *unspeakables.* It has been said that the Maori native people of New Zealand, for example, judge the health and vigor of their groups by how many of the undiscussables they find. (The fewer, the better!) Today, we have HR (Human Resources) Surveys and EI (Employee Involvement) Assessments that tell us what is happening within our organizations, teams, and groups. Knowing the health of an organization is paramount; that is, knowing whether the feedback systems are open, whether information is flowing freely, and whether leaders are in tune with actively addressing concerns.

There are two primary reasons why undiscussables go unaddressed: it may be because of the lack of courage to lift them up, or the lack of safety required to bring them forward to get resolved.

We all can connect to Hiney and hidden elephants just like him. Hiney, the elephant, is present when we learn about the new procedure being implemented for which there was no input, and none is solicited now. Hiney is present when we move forward to a new subject without completing the last (for the third time), by which we know something strange requiring silence is present. Hiney is present when we know that full disclosure is not happening or when something that was supposed to have been done by now has not been done, and, while excuses are rampant, the accountability for it remains unassigned. Silence prevails; the veil covering the elephant is not allowed to be lifted.

Note: Some people are quick to add that it is "lack of time" that hinders or prevents making elephants visible. That, for the most part, is an excuse, not a reason. See Chapter 8 for details about elephants and time.

TuSK...TuSK...TuSK:

It takes a ton of denial...
It takes a sprinkle of fearfulness too...
To keep *feeding* the elephants!

Avoiding conflict? Is that what we're doing?
Ahh, if only the conflict could be embraced
And resolved constructively...
We could then all move on!

Chapter 5:
Introducing Iney,
the Mostly-Invisible Elephant

Elephant-speak:

Iney is an elephant too. But she's a bit different than Hiney. That is because she is mostly invisible, but not always. Iney wears a magic cloak that she can take off whenever she wants—if she wants to become visible, and if she thinks you genuinely want to see her. Iney, for example, is willing to make herself visible when you leave that meeting room and go into the ladies' room. Then Iney, the mostly-invisible elephant, throws off her magic cloak and becomes visible just for a brief period of time—long enough to be recognized and talked about—usually with much disdain. Then, Iney turns invisible again as she dons her cloak once more. Life goes on…nothing's changed. Except we know that Iney the mostly-invisible elephant has allowed her name to be shared; more than one person is aware of her existence. She's also lifted up an emotion about her—all of which was uncovered in that ladies' room.

As we enter the meeting room again, we ponder: will Hiney the elephant (always hidden in our meetings) ever become like Iney? It happens again at the water cooler, outside of the hierarchical meeting setting. Iney, the mostly-invisible elephant, becomes uniquely visible again—just for a short while. We hear whispers about her because she's named. Sometimes Iney shows up at happy hours and coffee breaks too. She has even been known to show up on the golf course and ride along in the golf cart! Her name remains a *whispered name.*

Business-speak:

There is an unwritten rule for the times when we are in the presence of hidden elephants like Hiney. That rule generally is, "Silence—because it may not be safe." Yet, when we are in the presence of an Iney, the unwritten rule is more relaxed. We can talk about Iney, but only for brief moments and just in hushed tones. It is a bit uncomfortable to be fully seeing her or speaking her name, even in a whisper. There is another important factor happening that we sense as true—an inner knowing, and that is: to uncover our elephants—to get beyond the whispers—is going to take *Courage* (with a capital *C*).

Built into the ongoing saga of *elephants hiding in our midst* is the notion that our failure to acknowledge them—to be able to name our elephants, to make them visible, to lift them up so they can be addressed—is hurting our business, our organization, our work-team, our work-group. *The presence of elephants detracts from our being the best that we can be.* That necessary Courage (with a capital *C*) must be found. At a deep level, we know this. Effective leaders know that finding that courage, and authentically moving forward, recognizing the risk, has to happen.

Conflict avoidance (letting elephants stay hidden) is real in many organizations, businesses, teams, and work groups. Avoiding conflicts (pretending, ignoring) negatively impacts on productivity, morale, teamwork, and, ultimately, on your organization's bottom line. Yet constructive conflict resolution can actually be healthy for an organization. Conflict produces change. Conflict leads to unity. Addressing rather than suppressing conflict opens the lines of communication and gets people talking to each other instead of about each other. Conflict resolution promotes collaboration. People can learn how to work harmoniously, come up with creative solutions, and reach outcomes that benefit everyone—if they want to!

TuSK…TuSK…TuSK:

Can you see the elephants now?
There's an invisible herd in your organization!
Look closer! Each one does have a name!
Don't be afraid…look under the rug…be Courageous!

Oh, the environment doesn't permit it, you say?
It's not safe to name the elephant that you know is there?
So that means we keep right on…just keeping on…
Trudging on…smelling the elephant dung?

We see the smoke,
We catch a glimpse in the mirror,
We know all is not as it purports to be,
We know that all is not well from the whisper.

Smoke & Mirrors

Chapter 6:
Courage…the Elephant and the Mouse

Elephant-speak:

Most people have seen a cartoon or heard the urban legend that elephants are afraid of mice. Perhaps that is because we elephants have poor eyesight, yet have acutely sensitive hearing, so elephants can become easily frightened when we hear something rustling around us or under the rug, but cannot see what is there. It seems strangely upside-down to see the image of a giant, powerful elephant cowering in the corner, afraid of a squeaky little mouse—doesn't it?

Question: If you were an elephant and you were hiding comfortably under the rug, not expecting to be disturbed, what would be the one thing you'd be startled by—that one thing for which you might not be ready?

Could it be that someone—yes, someone—might find the courage and find a reasonable way to make one of us elephants visible? To lift up the rug without getting other people upset? To expose one of us elephants so that we could be dealt with in an effective, non-threatening way? To stop feeding the elephant with dinners of denial?

Answer: Expose the elephant—and do it diplomatically.

One at a time is just fine.

(No need to start a stampede!)

Business-speak:

There are several great business guidelines for elephant-hunting.

The first is promoting transparency. Transparency implies openness, communication, and accountability. Transparency is operating in such a way that it is easy for others to see what actions are performed. When transparency is a high value for an organization, a business, a work-team, or a work-group, there are few places for elephants to hide.

The second is possessing *managerial courage.* Having managerial courage means being able to stand up and appropriately, maturely, and diplomatically say what needs to be said at the right time, to the right person, in the right manner, with the right impact, in the right way. This is not done aggressively; rather, it is an assertive approach. This contains no meanness, no hostility; rather, it is based on clear principles—intended to move the organization or group or team forward. It can be done in a meeting or in private with the person most connected to the elephant that is under the rug.

The third is a strategy for safely lifting up the elephant by specifically and purposely using "I wonder" language. For example,

- I wonder if there is something under the rug that we're pretending not to notice?

- I wonder if anyone else sees what I see, and senses that we need to explore this more. I sense that we're ignoring a major concern. Does anyone else sense this?

- I wonder if anyone else recognizes that we haven't begun to lift up what is really at stake here; I'm wondering if anyone else sees what I see.

- I wonder if anyone sees a pattern happening here; I wonder if anyone else senses that we cover this each week, yet we're not dealing with the real issue. I wonder…does anyone else want to delve deeper into this to resolve this for the long term?

Then, wait…yes, *wait…with a very, very long pause* until someone else in the room answers. And soon, very soon, the elephant is "named." If by chance, no one answers, and everyone looks down, then simply say, "I guess this silence tells me we've got a real hidden elephant here, but we're just not ready to peek under the rug." It won't take long; soon there will be visits to your office by those who want to tell you all about the elephant they think is there, but they didn't have the wherewithal to raise it up in the room.

> "The most valuable thing any of us can do is find a way to say the things that can't be said."
>
> ~ *Susan Scott*

TuSK…TuSK…TuSK:

Come here, Elephant! I see you!

I know you're right here in this room with us.

I know your name too.

I wonder, colleagues, do you see this elephant too?

You do? Wonderful! Let's address it now!

You don't? Or…you don't want to?

What's the meaning of this *silence*?

Hmmm. I think this elephant just got bigger!

No worries. Soon it will fester and then, eventually, you'll see it too!

Chapter 7:
Hunting for Elephants

C. Stoelting

Elephant-speak:

So you know that, just as there are good leaders and not-so-good leaders, there are also good and not-so-good elephants. Yes, indeed. When you go elephant-hunting, you are looking for both the positive and the negative in the elephants that you find. Because there are both positive and negative elephants throughout your organization, your business, your work-team, your work-group, your office, and the shop floor. You are just not seeing them—or perhaps you're ignoring their presence.

You are right in the midst of things. You know when things seem right. You know when things seem not-right. You know when you smell a stinky elephant. You know when something good happens over and over and over again, and yet no one seems to notice, except, perhaps, you.

Most times, the elephants you are hunting are stinky elephants. That's because we stinky ones are destructive elephants that really do need to be found and addressed, because, directly or indirectly, we are hurting your organization or team and are detracting from your ability to be most successful. But there is another kind of elephant, too; an elephant that has a real sense of goodness about it—yet it gets lumped into the elephant story because, like the negative ones, people tend to *ignore* it. It is an elephant that no one chooses to talk about—but it is a good elephant! And that goodness shouldn't be continually ignored.

Think about the times that something good happens over and over again—a pattern that repeats, yet goes unrecognized, unheralded, unnoticed. Can you see that? Can you see those pockets in your organization that always deliver on time, on budget, with a smile? Can you name that pattern and share why it is a good pattern? There's an elephant in that pattern—something good that is happening over and over again, yet this elephant is not named—is virtually ignored. And accordingly, your organization or team misses out on great learning opportunities.

Conversely, how many times have you seen something negative (the elephant you keep grumbling about) happen? Can you see a pattern? (For example, the pattern of the elephant you know is hiding under the rug. How many times have you sensed it was there, yet said nothing?)

If you really want to find the elephants in your midst: look for the patterns! It is the patterns that your senses first notice. What have you become aware of?

You already know why we are hiding (right now) under the rug!

Business-speak:

Business is about performance. If you do not achieve the desired results, your business, organization, work-group, or work-team will cease to exist, or, at a minimum, will be labeled as ineffective. Accomplishing whatever it is your business, organization, work-group, or work-team is chartered to do, then, is *the key to measuring its success.* Built into that measurement are, not only the final results, but also the manner of accomplishing those results—the way you interacted with each other. You are in business, in an organization, in academia, in government to accomplish your work in the most effective ways you can (together). Basic Business Effectiveness 101: Enhance what is good. Address and resolve whatever is detracting from your success, from being the best you can be together.

An organization, a work-team, a work-group is made up of people.

People have to communicate in order to work together. So communication is important. When elephants have become embedded in our organizations, work-groups, or work-teams, you'll see patterns happening—that either help the team to get better at what they've come together to accomplish, or take away from being the best the team can be. *Observation is key.*

When you have discovered a positive pattern in your organization, your business, your work-team, or your work-group, it needs to be recognized and enhanced. For example, consistently good win-win team interactions are strengths.

When you have discovered a negative pattern in your organization, your business, your work-team, or your work-group, it needs to be recognized and addressed. Resolve it for the long term. For example, bullying tactics have negative impacts. Another example is recycling issues: What is it that causes things to have to often be recycled, rather than resolved? What's the pattern that is happening?

Honestly, openly, and diplomatically leveling with each other is important.

The problem named, is the problem solved! The stroke of appreciation given, spurs the next good deed.

Leaders can learn how to lift up the patterns and deep processes that are running in their respective organizations and institutions, uncover and address "the unspeakables," and create coherence in the organization while building on the strengths of people. *Shifting the culture to include the process for finding elephants makes a huge difference in effectiveness.*

TuSK...TuSK...TuSK:

I'm naming the Elephants I see,
I'm naming the Elephants I sense,
Good ones and Not-so-good ones.
And Yes! I now know what to do with each!

Chapter 8:
Elephants and Time

Elephant-speak:

We elephants are very, very patient. Elephants can live for a very, very long time. Once we get comfortable in the room, or under the rug, we can hunker down and wait patiently to be discovered.

We know that people are busy. We know that it takes a certain amount of agitation to motivate a person or a leader to decide to look under the rug to find us, to give us a name, and to make us visible.

We can wait…for a long while. After a period of time, however, we begin to get stinky—so that's why staying hidden for a long time is not good. The longer we stay hidden, the more your organization, work-group, or work-team is being negatively impacted—*you collectively are being less than you can be. (And we know that you know that too.)*

Elephants know what is going on in the minds of the people in the room. We can sense the things that people are telling themselves internally, like: *No time…not a good time…no time to do it now…no time left for this.…another time.…let somebody else find time to dig into this…*

We know that all of these types of time-phrases that people tell themselves when they're sensing there is an elephant nearby are part of the excuse jargon for *not* going elephant hunting. We know that they are *choosing to continue to ignore us for a while,* preferring that we just stay covered up, under the rug, until some other time! A more convenient time!

As elephants hiding under the rug, we also know what happens when leaders decide to *continually* ignore us. People around them notice and begin to whisper things like: "A leader is supposed to lead; if he/she won't or can't lead, then he/she should get out of the way!" The words of weakness start to percolate, albeit in whispers—more whispers!

Business-speak:

Time is money. Time can be expensive—especially when our time is not well-spent. People are busy. There is always more work to do than there is time to do it. Accordingly, prioritization happens. We do what we determine to be most important. We put our energy and effort into that which we decide is most important. We are discerning. Sometimes we must focus on the immediate; other times, we focus on the longer-term. Each is important to the success of the business, work-group, or work-team.

There is a fundamental truth when it comes to time. *You have enough time for anything you want to do—so long as it ranks high enough among your priorities.* When it comes to finding our hidden elephants, savvy leaders know that if they don't find and address their elephants quickly, delaying will ultimately cost them more—more effort, more energy, more time, more internal problems, and probably more expense.

Elephants are in our midst, and we have to find our elephants, similar to determining which of our battles we'll fight next. *And therein lies the duty: we must find the elephants…the sooner the better.* It may not be today that we choose to lift one up. It may not be immediate on one's calendar. It may be appropriate to wait until next week. But letting the elephants fester is a detriment to one's success and to one's reputation as a leader. Lifting up the elephants—making them visible—only takes a little bit of time. (Sometimes it is as easy as just asking one question!) What needs to happen to address one elephant or several elephants for the longer term? Creating and following through on that "what" may take longer, and for that you can plan. Until you name the elephant/s, though, nothing gets resolved. That is what is at stake when "no time" is used as the excuse.

In sum, leaders are chartered to make the time to look—to decide that it is important to know, for the longer-term health of the organization, team, or work-group, what those elephants are and to know what is at stake. *Organizations that include a process for elephant hunting know that their investment of time in doing this pays off in the long run.*

> **"Courage doesn't always roar. Sometimes courage is the quiet voice at the end of the day saying, 'I will try again tomorrow.'"**
> **~ Mary Ann Radmacher**

Make sure tomorrow comes!

TuSK…TuSK…TuSK:

Elephants are in our midst.
We know that we can make the time to find them!
Time is expensive and so we prioritize…
We can manage those things that we decide upon
    …to take up our time and energy.
We know that every minute counts…
And we know that every single person and
    every single leader
    has the same amount of time.
It is up to each of us….how much we choose to use…
….to find our waiting elephants!
If not today, then tomorrow…
and this tomorrow must come!

Chapter 9:
Elephants Travel Well-Worn Paths

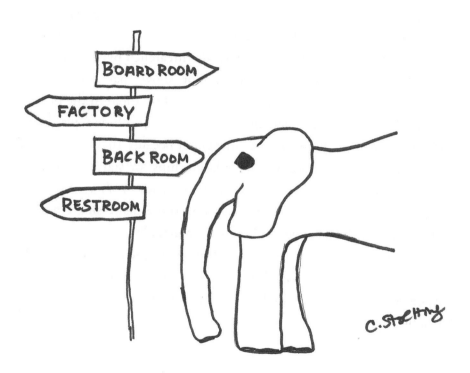

Elephant-speak:

Elephants are creatures of habit! We don't like change. We like to get comfortable under the rug, and just "be" there. While we are hoping to become discovered at some point, overall, we don't really like disturbance. Our well-worn elephant paths portray the status quo. We mostly like it like that! We like *just being comfortable* and playing our existence game—awaiting discovery—whether it is on our well-worn paths to the boardroom, the back room, or the restroom.

It has been said many times, that *people* are creatures of habit too—that people do not like change either. In fact, it is said that people resist change. They, like elephants, are actually threatened by change.

There have been many studies that show that people, when forced to change, or when change is imposed on them in the business world, for example, will actually hunker down and hide—just like us elephants. Strangely, people are threatened because they fear a loss of some sort—a loss of security, or relationships, or status, or control. And people play out that *sense of being threatened by change* by getting angry, fearful, distrustful, and uncertain. Those distressing emotions, of people resisting change in big ways, can actually transform into new elephants—more elephants that need to be discovered and resolved!

The larger our elephant line gets, the more in number we are, the more well-worn our paths become! And that means your elephant troubles are likely entrenched!

Business-speak

Change is inevitable. Change is the new normal. In business, change has been defined as an act or process in which something becomes different. There are many factors that can become an impetus for change—including environmental, social, political, economic, legal, or technological factors—and, of course, whatever changes we need to maintain our competitive edge. Business must succeed to stay in business. Business must make a profit today in order to be in business tomorrow. Otherwise, the doors close; that is the reality of the competitive marketplace.

Change is what it is—essential and integral to being in business.

Because change is happening, and because not all managers are skilled in collaborative consultation around change, and because sometimes change has to happen quickly—very quickly—often people will feel that the change is being imposed. That sets resistance into high-impact mode.

The challenge for leaders is to be able to lead through change—even imposed change—in such a way that morale is maintained, productivity continues, and people feel that their concerns have been heard and that someone understands them. Leaders can inspire others to move forward towards new, changed goals. This is a tall order.

Yet this is precisely what separates impactful leaders from managers. Effective leaders deal with change head-on and *rally resilience;* most managers deal with the status quo. Leaders know there are effective ways for making change in organizations—important processes to use that result in key, remarkable outcomes.

Leaders can learn to lead change in their organizations without contributing to the hidden elephant population—if they want to—without contributing to elephant path-making!

TuSK…TuSK…TuSK…

The elephants walk well-worn paths,
They're connected tail-to-tail,
Creatures of habit,
   not liking change,
   happy with the status quo.

In organizations, we've been known
   to contribute to the population
   that's growing under the rug…
In part because we know not how
   to effectively handle
   all the resistance to change.

Chapter 10:
Safety in Elephant-Lifting

Elephant-speak:

Sometimes people avoid saying what needs to be said because they are afraid of potential repercussions. They are afraid that the consequences for doing so will be detrimental. The environment for lifting up elephants is not considered safe.

You might be scolded, rejected, or punished (salary or position or potential tenure impacted).

You might not be heard with the good intentions you'd expected, thus you end up, perilously, *in the doghouse,* with relationships strained even further.

Have you ever thought about this—if you can see and smell an elephant in the room, why is it that others cannot?

Sometimes—believe it or not—*those closest to the elephant can't see it or smell it.* That's because they're actually too close to it! Yes! Too close to the problem to see it! Oh, one might be able to see the trunk, and another only the foot, and another the tail...and that's why they say that sometimes it is really hard to describe an elephant! That's why there are varied perceptions of what the elephant is and why it is so difficult to name us. And that's what helps us elephants to stay "under the rug" even longer! That's what makes "lifting up the elephant" difficult.

Business-speak:

Healthy conversations are ones that search for the truth. Interrogating reality is part of being in business. Organizations that are healthy, learning organizations are able to tackle their toughest challenges *together*. Leaders who are aware of the potential existence of hidden elephants know that not only must elephants be acknowledged, but that the leader has to be ready and open to lift it—address it—regardless of who it is that first recognizes the elephant's presence.

Healthy organizations know about *creating the safe zone bowl*—a safe gathering place, where the organization's or business's identity and their frame of reference can be continually examined, where information (and changing information) is openly shared, where relationships are valued, and where time is taken to ensure this safe-zone, focused, in-the-bowl interaction regularly happens.

Putting the elephant's name into the safe zone bowl is an important discipline for promoting the health of your organization, your group, or your workplace.

We don't always see what others see. Sometimes elephants are camouflaged. That's why purposefully inquiring into others' views, having built-in feedback systems, regularly reflecting and utilizing elephant-lift-up sessions are important to organizations and teams. Sensing mechanisms are key. Note: This does not mean holding bitch and tattle sessions; rather, this is about genuinely lifting up the real, deeper issues—the ones that, if resolved, can move your organization, your business, your team, your group forward to achieve whatever it is you came together to accomplish in the first place, and much more effectively!

Lifting up, identifying, dissecting, and fully understanding our elephants (our undiscussables) is important for enhancing the opportunity for the business, the organization, the work-team, or the work-group to be more successful, more effective, and more profitable.

Sometimes an organization will choose to utilize an HR survey to find the hidden elephants. The danger with this in an already-unsafe environment is that seldom are the surveys conducted in such a way that people truly feel safe in lifting up the hidden elephant—and that is because confidentiality is often compromised. Someone is "called out" for what he/she had the audacity to share. That's the big danger. Survey administrators must be able to deal with the elephant that is raised in a safe way. People see through HR surveys and often consider them very manipulative. *It is better to have the leaders in charge be fully able to lift up their own elephants without having to find out through the back door.*

TuSK…TuSK…TuSK:

> The elephants come marching one by one,
> The elephants come marching two by two,
> Now we know how to lift them up, one by
>   one and two by two,
> Ask…and quickly they are perceived,
> Ask…and soon they are fully revealed,
> Name them…and they are soon resolved!

Chapter 11:
Call for Help!

Elephant-speak:

Have you ever been in a situation where you can come up with a great idea or solution for someone else, but just can't seem to solve your own elephant problem? It is easier to talk about the elephants that you believe belong to others than it is to address some of your own—the ones you're stymied about what to do next. We can be blind to our own elephants.

This happens in organizations, teams, and groups. You can smell, sense, or see an elephant clearly, and know just what to do about it. Others may be totally in denial. Others may sense the problem but lack courage to face it as it is—they prefer to dress it up, put it in a circus tuxedo, dabble it with perfume, and pretend it is not an elephant. It is easier sometimes to just let it be. Still, the elephant is an elephant, even if you are too close to the problem to see it clearly, or when you're in a discouraging or unsafe environment, or when you're just plain stymied by what to do about your own elephant, let alone the organization's elephants.

When you can't lift up and address your own elephant, or when your organization can't lift up and resolve its own herd of elephants, then it is time to *call for help!*

Business-speak:

A recent study by researchers revealed that when people solved problems on behalf of others, they produced faster and more creative solutions than they did when they solved the same problems for themselves. (E. Polman, NYU & K Emich, Cornell, 2011).

This may help to explain why *an outside expert* is often most effective for helping organizations, their leaders, teams, or groups to see problems and elephants they hadn't been able to see, and to effectively elicit the information that needs to be lifted up—while creating a safer environment—so that resolutions can be found quickly. Thus, the organization moves forward, with greater rigor and discipline; with better health and vitality. Why? Because the *undiscussables* have been transformed into *discussables*. The elephants have been lifted up, named, and addressed for the betterment of the organization, business, group, or team.

This also explains why many struggling entrepreneurs/solopreneurs/small business owners join Mastermind groups where they can safely air their concerns and receive a wealth of advice and confidence for addressing their business situations. Others can see what you may not be able to see.

Is it time you called for help? Is it time to acknowledge your elephants?

TuSK...TuSK...TuSK:

Elephants are great teachers
   for organizations and leaders.
When you learn to lift up and face your elephants
   they disappear...no longer lumps in the rug.
Sometimes, though, you need some help,
   And that is absolutely *okay* too.
Sometimes we're reluctant to change,
   We like our well-worn path,
So calling for help to help us out,
   Is exactly the facilitation we need.

Chapter 12:
There's a Whole Herd of Elephants in Your Organization

Elephant-speak:

What's in a name? We elephants in the room and under the rug are always noticing the people who are in the room—even though they can't see us. We have categories for those people in the room. And what we've noticed is that almost always, the people in the room follow a progressive pattern around garnering courage to speak up and find us under the rug…and it is generally tied to their level of frustration. Courage seems to start with a little *c* and progress to the big *C*. The ones who consistently let us get really comfy-cozy and become long-term residents we mostly call "wimps" (for currently lacking the *w*ill to find *imp*ortant *s*olutions). Those people whom we can tell are getting agitated and are definitely smelling our presence, we mostly call "dimps" (for *d*aringly close to finding *imp*ortant *s*olutions). While we elephants are always ready with our category names for people, it seems so strange to us that people have such difficulty naming us—their hidden elephants.

And what do we call those people who diplomatically pull back the rug, uncover the elephants, lift us up, and get us addressed? We honor them by calling them *"C-Ls"*—meaning leaders who are specially gifted with both the **C**apacity to **L**ead and who also possess **C**ourage to **L**ead with a capital *C*. Elephants always honor the leader, and we especially honor C-Ls. Are you a C-L? Are you that special leader with great courage and the capacity to lead—to find us and then come up with the right remedy to resolve the elephant problem?

Business-speak:

In review,

- Elephants within the organization (or work-team, work-group, or business) *are anything (big or little) that people can't or won't talk about or are hugely uncomfortable in raising up.* Sometimes elephants are ignored because to do otherwise would cause great embarrassment, would trigger confrontations, or is simply considered taboo.

- An *elephant in the room* can represent a person, a behavior, an assumption, an idea, an element of performance, a situation, a problem, an issue, a thing, a condition, a conflict, the status quo, political correctness, a social taboo, and more!

- To go elephant-hunting in organizations takes leadership, exemplified by effective leaders, regardless of role or position; courage to speak up is essential. It is true that many people, including leaders, will hold back if they think that in some way they will be "disadvantaged" if they speak up. The roots of this aversion to risk come from the basic tendency of human nature to ask, "How will this impact me?" *Being able to maturely and diplomatically raise up the elephant issues for the betterment of the organization becomes a key definer of true leadership.*

When a leader and his/her team *choose to change their culture for the better,* it means a decision has been made that things cannot be as they were—the team must do things differently in order to have something different and better. There are many culture change frameworks that leaders can utilize with their teams to move forward effectively. Change management means…shifting the way we manage, lead, and collectively do things. There are important team competencies that correspond to shifting the culture. One, for example, is ridding the team of defensiveness (which so often leads to conflict and derisiveness).

An organization can shift to a culture that openly finds its elephants. Effective leaders know that it doesn't have to be that same old way—the way that harbors hiding elephants!

TuSK...TuSK...TuSK:

Is it any wonder why it is so hard to describe
an elephant in the room? Or under the rug?
Perhaps we'll try an HR survey...
But oh my, whatever will we do with what we find out?
Do we really want to know?
Will we really address those elephants we find?
Do we have the skills? The wherewithal?
Can we shift the way we lead and manage...
To a different culture? A different, better place?
Yes!

Chapter 13:
Why Won't People Talk About Elephants Openly?

Elephant-speak:

Q: Why won't people talk about us elephants openly?

A: Because they are afraid.

Q: What do they fear?

A: There are many different types of fear:

- Fear of raising questions about the status quo.

- Fear of speaking up and not getting support.

- Fear of telling the truth. (Per the old story about the emperor who thinks he's wearing clothes but in reality, he is not!)

- Fear of challenging, especially when there are perceived bullies in the room.

- Fear of disadvantaging oneself in the moment, and for the future.

- Fear of appearing critical of higher-ups.

- Fear of being perceived as just wanting to make waves.

- Fear of being ridiculed.

- Fear of being criticized, humiliated, diminished, or shamed.

- Fear of various ramifications (perceived or real).

So, can you imagine how big the *elephant herd* must be in an organization or work-team that is a hostile environment in which to work? People can't talk/won't talk because of the environment of fear. In a hostile environment it is deemed unsafe to challenge the status quo. To *transform* to a workplace that has few elephants means that leaders have to step in, step up, and embark on a *culture-changing shift*. The new culture has to become one where finding and naming elephants becomes a safe way of life—the valued way to be and to do business—every day.

In elephant-speak, we call this *carpet cleaning!*

Business-speak:

It doesn't have to be that way!

Leaders can be elephant-lifting leaders at any level of an organization—even within the hostile environments. Start with your immediate circle of influence. Set in place safe conditions so that people can stand up and say diplomatically that there is an elephant in the room that needs to be addressed. Leaders can show that they are also willing to lead the process of lifting an elephant up so it can be safely addressed. Asking for others to support the uncovering of elephants that are keeping your group from being the best it can be is a noble business endeavor, and, in itself, is a strong principle on which to stand.

Note: Some business people, including the author, have had the experience of seeing where one person, a truly effective leader, yet not the one at the top, profoundly influenced the culture of his work-team, then his department, then a whole division. He was a valid elephant finder! His organization became the best at what they were chartered to do! He was a C-L!

Leadership is so very, very important for creating the conditions where providing feedback is safe, where the truth can safely be told and is expected, where reality is interrogated, where focusing on finding the elephants is an important part of doing business. This is principle-centered, integrity-based leadership.

TuSK...TuSK...TuSK:

Leaders...are you listening?

C-Ls...are you out there?

Courageous leaders....are you standing up?

Leaders with the Capacity to Lead....are you ready?

On what guiding principles do you stand?

Chapter 14:

It Is Not Fun to Clean Up After an Elephant... so It Is Best to Find Them and Address Them Before They Take Up Residence!

Elephant-speak and Business-speak...on the same track:

Can you see them now?

Simple Things You Can Do to Find the Hidden Elephants

Observe. When there's heavy stress evident in your meeting room and attendees have gone quiet, when breathing gets shallow, when body language shows tightness, there's an elephant lurking. When silence is noticeable, when there's a reluctance for people to speak, there's an elephant lurking. (Ask: Why?)

Stop and ask everyone to breathe, and take a short break. Upon re-gathering, share that it is time to name the elephant that's in the room. (Sometimes using Post-it notes to write down identifying clues about the elephant affords a better comfort-level than directly speaking up.) Base this request on the genuine desire to lift up this elephant so that your organization or team can ultimately become better than it is right now.

When whispering is happening around the water-cooler, eavesdrop and pointedly *ask* to be let in on the "whisper subject." You'll know by the response whether you need to dig deeper. (There's generally an elephant present.)

C-Ls are open to raising questions like:

- What are we pretending not to see or not to know?

- What question/s are we avoiding?

- What is the most important question for us to work on?

- What actions should we be taking that we are not? (Why is that?)

- Why won't we interrogate reality? What's real and what's not?

- Where does our reluctance to address something show up?

- Why are we afraid to bring this up?

- What seems to happen over and over again with not-so-good results?

- What are we grumbling about over and over again?

- What's being talked about in the break room that isn't talked about in the meeting room? Why is that?

- What principled behaviors do we expect? How have we communicated this? And how do we reinforce this?

- Is there a lie or a misconception or a misunderstanding or a misalignment that we've bought into? How does that happen?

- Everyone is unusually quiet and withdrawn. Why is that?

- Is there an elephant we need to address?

- What is it that we really want to have happen? And why is that outcome so difficult for us? What are we afraid of?

- Why is it that, when a positive gesture has genuinely been put forth, it is met with a negative response? What is feeding that negativity?

Use "I wonder...." language to gently lift up the first glimpse of the elephant. (Refer back to Chapter 6.)

Use the "crumple-the-crushing-elephant—then-really-toss-it-around" method. Have everyone *identify the elephant in the room, name it, and describe it* as best they can on a sheet of paper. You may need to pose several direct questions, or you might be searching for something specific, for example: *What specifically needs to take place to achieve the outcomes we need to accomplish here together?* Then instruct the participants to crumple up that piece of paper and toss it into the center of the room, or the table. Then each person pulls out a crumpled sheet (other than their own) and reads it aloud. After all the papers have been read, ask the group to collectively summarize what came out—to best describe this elephant so it can be addressed for the betterment of the team, the group, the organization, the business. Everyone should be provided a chance to describe the collective elephant. Post the summary statements as the group together lifts up the elephant; the elephant is made visible. This method is a very quick way to lift up the elephants, and to do it in an effective, safe way.

Be genuine. Be sure you will address the elephant once it is raised up. Transparency includes Openness, Communication, and Accountability. When genuineness is not present, people see through it; not trusting follow-through, being a bully to get things your way, or being a con-artist are all elephants in themselves. Think about HR surveys that fail. Why? Because people opened up and shared information—many at personal peril and professional risk—yet little was done to improve the situation. As you move forward, slowly, remember the old adage: *How do you eat an elephant? One bite at a time.* Keep moving forward, uncovering the elephants *genuinely.*

At the conclusion of every meeting, high-level or low-level, take the time to deeply reflect on the meeting content and process. This is not a reflection-by-rote, such as: *good meeting, kept to time, leader did a great job.* The reflection to request is much deeper, such as: *What is the elephant in the room that hindered us from being the best we could be together, or from addressing our business for the best outcome?* Each time this is done, the organization, the team, the work-group will become stronger and more open to lifting up the elephants.

Call your direct reports or your team together and share this elephant story. Work on the principles, standards, and behaviors that you, as a team, need to understand and commit to in conducting your business, in genuinely lifting up your elephants, and in interacting with each other. Once these are firm, post them in your meeting room, signed off by each person. And each week, have each person provide a number score from 1 to 10 on how well you interacted together against those principles, standards, elephant-lifting behaviors, etc. Talk openly about what your number means, and talk deeply about the reasons behind the numbers. No one can dispute another's number (ground rule). Chart the numbers graph. (No personal attacks. Just the facts.) As time moves forward, this visible exercise will help you to find and address your elephant issues.

Hold an Elephant Focus Group with a cross-section of the organization, for the purpose of "Organizational Sensing." The group is chartered with uncovering what needs to be uncovered, and the leader needs to be part of this, to lend credibility and transparency. One caveat: Lifting up an elephant may generate undesirable behaviors; be clear in your ground rules that being open and honest does not provide a license to be mean or cruel. Rather, the group is chartered with lifting up the primary elephants that are crushing your organization. Addressing them can help your organization to be the best that it can be (together), and accomplish the best that it can do (together). (Again, no personal attacks; just the facts.)

The military has long had a practice of doing After-Action-Reviews (AAR)*, a disciplined approach providing candid insights into specific strengths and weaknesses from various perspectives, providing feedback and insight critical to improved performance, and providing details often lacking in evaluation reports alone—all of which is applicable to finding elephants in organizations. By adopting AAR, you can enable a group of people to gain new insights from shared experiences, which can, in turn, be applied to the task at hand. The basic questions are: What was expected to happen? What actually occurred? What went well, and why? What was expected to happen that didn't happen, and why? What can be improved, and how? This is a process done best with a facilitator. The intent is to provide an expanded perspective and to learn—to prevent that next elephant from taking up residence! *Given what we learned, how can we now apply these insights to what we do next?*

(*Note: Google *After Action Review* to find multiple entries for facilitating this step-by-step improvement process.)

The Fish Bowl is an interactive, yet focused, approach that can be used for learning—for lifting up both the negative, more destructive elephants, and also for lifting up the good, but overlooked, elephants.

This Fish Bowl works especially well when a new leader or team has the "position of power" and people in the group are not sure of his/their intent, background, expectations, plans, concerns, or changes that he/they have in mind. It involves a safe interview-like process. Someone, or perhaps a panel of two or three people, sits in the middle of the circle (usually a semi-circle) and is asked to expound on a number of deep questions put forth by either a skilled moderator or interviewer—one who can ensure safety. The questions focus on: what's happening, the view of the situation, business, group interactions, behaviors, intent to become better at what the organization is trying to do, the elephants they see, etc. Those around the semi-circle are asked to listen carefully, as they will be summarizing the most meaningful pieces and the learning that came forth from this fish bowl, particularly pieces that they may not have realized before. The moderator phrases the questions for open-endedness, for getting the best thinking about: the why of things, historical perspectives, openness of the organization, necessity for change, elephants, good and not-so-good, and more. Those listening will also be asked, at the end, what still needs to happen for this group to move forward, and they may potentially identify even more elephants. The person or persons in the center are provided multiple iterations to clarify their input. The entire process is one of moving forward with much more openness and trust, and fewer elephants.

Simple Things to Do to Find the Softer (Positive) Elephants

Observation and Asking Questions are two important skills for finding Positive Elephants.

Ask your team to come prepared to the next meeting, or to send you in writing within a few days, answers to these types of questions:

- What happens over and over again with good results?

- Where are the pockets of excellence in our organization, or team?

- What can we learn from them? How can we build on them?

- What do they consistently do that makes for repeated good results?

- How can we recognize/enhance/increase/spread this?

And, very importantly...Why is it that we have not acknowledged this superb action previously? (Therein lies an elephant.)

Note: The process of Appreciative Inquiry* is an excellent way to lift up positive elephants. (*AppreciativeInquiry.case.edu/intro/whatisai.cfm)

Chapter 15:
Overcoming Elephant Angst (Examples)

C. Stoetting

Elephant-speak and Business-speak combined:

When it comes to elephants, we're in this together!

Here are some different examples of elephants that the author has found hidden under the rug and helped to lift up so they could be addressed and resolved.

An Egocentric Leader. This leader was unable to recognize the hostile environment created by his tirades and his overuse of command and control; thus, the fear-based culture of the organization, and poor results. He was afraid that if he did not dictate, then things would not be done the way he wanted them to be done. He saw the impact of the revolving door on his organization and read the feedback explaining why people actually left his organization; this elephant wasn't pretty.

(Often) Violating Chain of Command. A pattern of people going to the big boss, or to members of the Board of Directors, instead of their line organization *for their own personal gain,* thereby actively undermining the managerial leadership line. Game-playing is the elephant. All levels of this organization were contributing to the game. Making it transparent and setting in place the correct response at all levels was essential. Why? So that the organization could become the best they could be (together), thus serving their clients and constituents better—the very reason for being in business.

(Please note the word *often* above—which is entirely different than what might be expected to happen in a whistle-blowing situation.)

Us and Them. Polarized positions—to the point where in-fighting is such that the group has forgotten the purpose—the *why*—of being in business in the first place. What is the product or service you are rendering? What are the accomplishments required of the group, the difference between where you are now, where you want to be, and what must happen, including the professional behaviors exhibited among and between the members necessary to succeed most effectively? One question asked when such in-fighting takes root is this: why can't you choose peace? Therein lies the elephant.

Political Correctness/Social Taboos. Playing the race card, the gender card. A confrontation has started and the race or gender card is played, so discussion stops. People retreat. Everything stalls. Subject is changed.

That's when the group needs a facilitator and to be called together again. The entire situation needs to be drawn out, including all the facts, as well as noting when the race or gender cards were played and why. The big picture has to be made visible along with the timeline. The facts are what are most important. Often conflicts rest on the emotional tentacles, instead of the facts. The arena of defensiveness has to be defined at the very beginning, and the facilitator has to be able to discern, with the group, what is the intention, what is the objective they (the organization, the team) are trying to reach, and what other ways, what other possibilities are there? Asking the question, "How can it (the outcome) get better than this?" (because everyone in the room—together—is better than this) is a hugely important question to get answered to move forward beyond the entrenched elephants.

Not sticking with the Program. Ignoring the Plan of Action. One organization's leader was a wonderful idea-generator. Every idea had merit, and every idea that was voiced was expected to have follow-through. His subordinates could not keep up with his drum rolls, and some ideas actually countered earlier ones. The situation became chaotic and disorganized. Employees *could never get it right;* they never measured up to his changing plans and expectations. Was it any wonder why effectiveness and results weren't happening? Was it any wonder that there was high turnover?

Chronic lateness. Each week there is a special meeting that 7 people attend. The pattern is that 4 out of 5 times, the same person is late by 5 to 10 minutes. The pattern is this: the person enters the room, apologizes for being late, pulls out his chair, and sits down. The other meeting attendees notice his arrival, roll their eyes, then look down— waiting to see what the leader will do. The longer the leader waits to address the tardiness, the worse this elephant becomes. Over a number of months, the pattern has become cemented. The elephant is this: the leader is not doing his job. By his inaction in not calling the employee on his behavior, he has set a new standard— that is, that it is okay to be chronically late; that it is okay to disrespect your coworkers' time; that it is okay to have those who were at meetings on time repeat and recycle to bring the repetitive latecomer up to speed. Second, the other elephant is the tardy employee's behavior itself; what is necessary to happen in order for him to understand his selfishness, the value of punctuality, and respecting his coworkers' time? This example shows the need to address elephants promptly, before they dig in under the rug.

Unprofessionalism. Some organizations and teams have made it okay to be unprofessional in their dealings with each other, and even with clients or customers or academic colleagues. Usually there is a long litany of hurts and a trail of events, name-calling, back-stabbings, undermining, and overall bad behaviors. Unprofessionalism is an elephant that can be lifted up and exposed for precisely what it is. Once a light has been put on the specific behaviors and the connection made to the impact on the business, this elephant disappears quickly. Unprofessionalism does not like being exposed. An important follow-up is that clarity on the behaviors that are expected to be fully demonstrated going forward is key, along with agreed-upon consequences.

Inability to tell the truth. One governmental agency placed a high value on "not saying anything bad." That led to not saying what needed to be said for fear of hurting another person's feelings, and for not wanting to violate the unwritten niceness rule. Being constructively critical had been carelessly mixed in with destructive criticism. What this meant is that *people could not tell the truth.* Exposing this elephant for the long-term impact upon the work of, the reputation of, and value of the agency was important to do.

Pretending not to know. A Board of Directors of a not-for-profit pretended that they didn't have to think about what would happen (someday coming soon), when their organization's funding stream stopped, continually avoiding the subject; thus, they were unprepared when it happened, and they had to quickly reinvent themselves. This was a case of being stuck in the present status quo; avoidance of the issue; not able to interrogate reality. The elephant was always in the room with them.

Pretending not to know. An industrial plant's operational staff fully understood the changing seasons and the impact of bad weather upon outdoor operations. In their busyness, however, they failed to look ahead sufficiently and were "caught unprepared." One time would be bad enough. But having to shut down two years in a row because of being surprised by winter is bad business. There were several elephants in the room. Costs, overtime greed, feigning blindness to the situation, not using the learning process, tight schedules, reduced manpower. *Some elephants, when not addressed promptly, actually multiply—they beget new and more elephants.* In this situation, with a lack of leadership, the blame game became apparent as well. Maintenance blames Operations, Operations blames Maintenance. Then when that doesn't play well, it is First Shift had left it for Third Shift and the round-and-round blame game continues. Power plays to avoid taking responsibility, and other games people play can emerge like a chess match. The big, complex elephant can be lifted up by looking forward…Who is responsible now? At this moment? And what are you going to do next? And how will we all know that it is being completed? What accountability must be tracked? What will make this transparent?

The Cover-up. People don't like to be called out for doing something wrong, for being at fault for something. The cover-up elephant can be a close cousin of the blame game, this one played by not owning up, by pretending it didn't happen, by pointing a finger elsewhere, by creating confusion, by raising some doubts…anything to avoid having to take responsibility. Interestingly, when working with a group of counselors/teachers at a residential school, and while addressing the elephant in the room—for which the long, laborious, and inventive "couldn't be us…must be someone or something else" cover-up was well underway—there, right within this Kindergarten classroom, were the rules for moving forward together and getting beyond their elephant issue: Tell the Truth. Own up! (Take responsibility.) Play fair. Share. No hitting. Inside Voices. Behave…Follow the Rules. Be the Best You Can Be.

Going back on the agreed-upon plan. Agreeing to a plan (in the formal meeting setting)—then going and doing something else, and expecting that this was okay. The group had made it okay by not calling/naming the behavior the destructive, dishonest, elephant-confusion that it was. Also, meeting hijacking by bullies can fall into this scenario—not being challenged for the disturbance this causes—taking away from the greater potential of group success. In this case, there were no "agreed-to principles and standards" on which the group could stand. The elephant was found by getting the group to identify the issues and concerns that were holding the group back in their work and honestly addressing what needed to happen for the group to begin to move forward together, aligned and committed to new principles and accountabilities.

Performance. Each month a special organizational meeting was held to address safety performance on a plant site. Each month, certain reports became further behind. Each month this continued. Each month the list became longer and longer and longer. The elephant in the room was that no one would stand up and say, "Enough! This can't go on!" Everyone knew what was behind the non-performance. No one would speak to the leader about it because it was his area of oversight. This elephant in the room was a stinky, festering elephant. The implications of this could have impactful consequences.

Blind trust. When devotees are addicted to the leader and all the leader says and does. The old question—*Would you jump off the cliff if he told you to?*—fits here. There are organizations where trust is misplaced—where, if the leader says so, then no one differs from his opinion. Have you been in a room or meeting where everyone stays silent until they have heard the leader's opinion first? Perhaps the leader has set this environment and his word is all that matters.

Perhaps fear is plentiful. Blind trust devotees have learned that there is no room for challenging the leader's position or for growing the organization into greater maturity. This is a big elephant, yet it can be addressed. Holding up the mirror, looking at performance, and looking at why people stay or don't stay in this environment are key. A primary question, often overlooked, is: What does this leader really want? Do his espoused desires mesh with his values in practice? What is his behavior when his ideas/opinions are challenged?

Alliances. A large bank with multiple branches was expanding. A new manager was put in place with authority for all the managers at the branches. The branch managers, resisting this, conspired to undermine the new manager—wouldn't provide the reports requested, resisted at every turn, continually tried to discredit, became sophomoric in their behavior. They were excellent in creating smoke screens for masking this from upper management. The elephant in the room was obvious and smelly. Yet the bank leaders pretended not to see the behavior—after all, these were long-term branch managers. That new manager resigned with a fiery resignation letter. Then Manager #2 was hired for the position and the same behaviors came forth. Finally, that ugly elephant in the room was exposed. A Vice President, once he could now see the repetitive pattern, called the game. It was a big and destructive elephant to address, with multiple behavioral issues included.

The boss's son is not pulling his load. Everyone sees this—except the boss/owner and his son! Yet no one knows how to lift this up for the reality and truth that it is, without ramifications. By not pulling his load, the business is clearly not as good as it could be; sales are clearly slipping, yet no one will speak. The long-term health of the business is at stake. Can you see how the elephant was clearly present and continued to fester until it was lifted up for what it really was? The conversation was long overdue.

Reality check. A reality check was called for when an inter-group-agency-type organization was dependent on membership for growth, and was dying in place. Yet the current members and the officers could not or would not see their rigidity, only doing things one way—the very same way they'd been doing things for 20 years. Now, that doesn't fly in the modern electronic world, and certainly younger, tech-savvy women don't share that value or that way of conducting business. So the real message—even though they espoused that they wanted to grow their organization and get youth and more member agencies into it—what they really wanted to do was preserve their status quo. They were not open to change, and that means that the last one standing turns out the lights. Now some anchors, some turf pieces are just that strong. In this case, their behavior showed that exclusivity and status quo were what they really wanted. They were pretending not to see the reality and consequences of not changing. The elephant for this group was that what they espoused (needing to grow with new and younger people and organizations to survive) did not match their behavior (uncomfortable with change/resistance to modernize). This was a case of espoused values versus values in use.

Management by committee. A not-for-profit organization was struggling with effectiveness, primarily because they "managed by committee." The committees were not well-focused, not effectively trained in meeting-leading, nor timely in meeting their work deadlines. The group's agenda items languished; productivity was low. The result was that the Executive Team stayed in exasperation mode, unable to get ahead of the problems, mostly having to "wait on the committees." The elephant in the room was "politeness." It was not acceptable to call a committee to task or to infer that something was amiss; rather, everyone needed to be nice, because after all, the committees were all made up of volunteers, and every volunteer is important to the entity. This type of elephant begets more elephants because when an organization is "too nice"—unable to instill, require, and find ways for expectations to be met—then back-door allegations begin. What won't be said to one's face, gets said through the back door. She said that he said that she said that he said…! Backbiting/backstabbing happens. Another elephant is now under the rug. A complete real-world, elephant-identifying meeting was necessary—highlighting the huge benefits and talents of volunteers, channeled now into new processes and accountabilities that meet the organization's deadlines so the organization can be even better at meeting the needs of the community it serves, and its volunteers can be heralded even more.

Dealing with the wicked problem. The wicked problem is a very sticky one—complex, with many tentacles, and difficult to address because of incomplete, contradictory, and changing requirements—often including multiple systems—business, community, employee, union—and with multiple impacts—social, political, economic. This is where the use of the Process Enneagram© tool (see References section at the end of the book) provides a way to see the complexity and allows what is most important to emerge for the group to connect with, and to then move forward. Sometimes that wicked problem is *the elephant that is so hard to describe*. It doesn't have to be that way.

Enough of the elephants!

Chapter 16:
The Roadmap (for Elephant Hunting) That Never Fails

Summary Notes

Chapter 14 provided several ways and means for leaders to begin to address their elephants (right now). Some are as simple as *observing* or *asking a simple question*, or phrasing what you think you see or know in *I wonder* language and waiting for your group's response.

Next, Chapter 15 provided some clear examples of elephants that have been found (and addressed) in organizations, businesses, work-teams and groups, by the author. Most leaders probably identify with these type examples—which also show how the hiding, lurking elephants and unresolved conflicts had negative implications on the respective organization. And more importantly, that finding and addressing those elephants made a huge difference for the on-going effectiveness of the group and their ability to move forward together. Thriving happens when the hidden elephants are found and addressed; and when a process is put into place so that new elephants can't get comfortable—they are noticed and addressed quickly.

This chapter (Chapter 16) provides insights into **The Roadmap (for Elephant Hunting) that NEVER Fails.** Consider this a process, a framework, or a model that always works! Yes, it works best if it is skillfully facilitated with a leader and his/her group as they all elephant-hunt together.[1] You can do this! Your group can do this! You can do

---

1   The roots of this model stem from complexity science as it applies to organizations and groups of people who interact toward achieving some purpose together. The scientific basis of Complexity as it applies to Leadership (and complex adaptive systems) is further detailed in books and articles written about Self-organizing Leadership and Complexity-related theories, including The Process Enneagram©... the Map that never fails. See Reference page.

this for the benefit of the whole group. You can get skilled facilitative help, if you need to. You can facilitate a meeting using this circular process and deep discussion—if you want to. No excuses! You can do this!

For the purposes of this *hidden elephant book*, know that the Roadmap process never fails…with one condition…and that is, that people are willing to talk openly—to truthfully interrogate reality. If people are closed to talk about their elephants, then their elephants will stay hidden and will continue to fester. If that is the case, then the largest lump under the rug is notable: the environment is too unsafe to speak up—the big hidden elephant continues to live on.…

It doesn't have to be that way! Those special Leaders (C-L's) with both the Courage and Capacity to Lead….can change things right now!

The Roadmap (for Elephant Hunting) that Never Fails is a simple circle, a continuous circle. [2]

(9-Term System; Process Enneagram©)

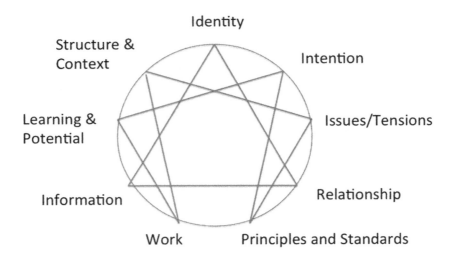

---

2   Process: There are **three** conversation levels in this process. The first is to follow the full perimeter in clockwise order…per the order of question examples that are shown specifically as first round questions. Do not proceed to the second round until you've completed the full circle of first round questions. The second round is to return to a discussion of Principles/Standards in connection to the Intentions at a second, deeper level; and the third is to return to a discussion of Principles/Standards—third level questions—while also looking again at Potential/Deep Learning and New Work that transforms your whole group. That's it! You've got it!

Getting Started: The Leader and the group (together) honestly address questions *like/similar to* the ones shown (for each category) on the following pages.

Remember, this is a sampling of questions to ask when a group genuinely wants to come together to address the larger issue of, **"How can we be the best that we can be together, be the most effective we can be, while openly addressing our elephants?"**

Identity-Type Questions:

- Who are we?

- How long have we been together?

- What is it that we are chartered to do?

- What has our performance been like?

- What roles do we perform? How do we all connect?

- How are we accountable to others?

- How do we fit in with the larger or smaller organization?

- Are we a team? What kind of a team? A cohesive team? A grumbling team? A "can-do" team, a "wait and see" team, an exemplary team? How do you know?

- How would others describe us, see us?

- If this team had a mantra, what would it be?

- What is the unwritten descriptor or motivator that runs deep about our team?

Intentions-Related Questions:

- What is it that we want to be able to do together successfully?

- What does success look like? Real, genuine success? Do we all see that?

- How do we want to be together as a group as we seek success?

- What are we ultimately responsible for?

- What are we chartered to do? Accountable for?

- What do we want to do better than we are doing?

- What would be a better way of being together than we currently are?

- What could we potentially accomplish together? What's the best we can be?

Issues/Tensions-Related Questions:

- What's getting in the way of achieving what we want to do?

- Why is that? (Can you name *whys* for each obstacle?)

- What are the elephants we don't want to talk about? Why is that?

- Why haven't we achieved our goals or exceeded them?

- What's happening that is bringing us down, dividing us, hampering our progress in all arenas—in what we do, in how we do it, in our processes, systems, in our behaviors with each other?

- What are the things we grumble about the most, complain about the most?

Relationships-Type Questions:

- How interdependent are we? (Or are we dependent? Or independent?)

- What behaviors are getting in the way of our accomplishments?

- Why have we not addressed our/this elephant before?

- Do we feel safe enough to talk, or not? If not, why not?

- Do we play win-win or win-lose with each other?

- Are there alliances that are detrimental, or bullies that are hindering us?

- Can we play fair together? Do we understand each other? Can we function as a team, or not? Is the team divided? Untrusting of each other? Holding back information? Playing favorites? Undermining? Supportive?

Principles & Standards-Related Questions:

First Round: (The values in use vs. espoused values.)

- What are the principles on which we do our work right now, really?

- On what do you individually and collectively stand?

- For what can you be counted on?

- On what do you pride yourselves?

- What principles or standards do you follow now to get work done?

Consider your answers to these questions and whether there are disconnects with answers you've already provided. For example, if there is discord in the team, or among factions that are hindering progress, then a principle of how you do your work right now of "we work together well" would be a disconnect. If you're not achieving your goals, then sharing a principle that "we do everything right on target" would be an obvious disconnect.

Second Round:

- If you really want to accomplish what you've shown as your true intentions, what has to change in order to accomplish them?

- In what new ways do you have to be together?

- In what different ways do you have to do things?

- Bottom line, what are the requirements and new commitments you'll need to have in order to truly achieve what you want to achieve (what you've not been able to achieve doing the things the way you've been doing them)?

- What differences in team interaction will be needed?

- What will have to be different?

- What new principles and standards will be necessary?

Third Round: (Discovering the real elephants.)

Knowing that if you don't change the *what* of what you're doing and you don't change the *how* of how you're doing things, then you'll end up with the same old results—the same elephants will remain under the rug.

- How committed are you to living by the new principles?

- How committed are you to achieving the intentions?

- How committed are you individually and as a team, to being held accountable to these new principles, new intentions?

- What are you afraid of that might derail you?

- How will you address this?

- How will living by these new principles show up?

- What will we all see?

- What measures do we need to ensure this happens?

- How will this be kept transparent?

- What will you have to stop doing? Start doing? Do more of? Do less of?

New Work:

First Round:

Describe the primary work your team engages in now. What is your purpose for being together? What do you accomplish? If things have emerged for you that show new work that is necessary for achieving your intentions, for building relationships, for addressing your elephants, please list those.

Second Round:

Describe the new work that has to be done by the leader and this group or team to fulfill the new intentions, address the real issues, set up the new accountabilities, build the relationships, and maintain transparency. (List the most important things first!) This will have emerged from the earlier discussions, and will be quite apparent. This answers the What-Why-Who-Where-When piece and sets up the accountabilities. Make this fully transparent, complete with visible accountabilities. (At a minimum, these three things are essential as part of the new work: that the map you've created is openly posted in your meeting room; that each time you meet, you spend 5 to 10 minutes talking about how you're doing per your commitments; and that you collectively hold each other accountable—you don't let any non-accountability elephants hide under the map!)

Information:

Describe the new information the leader/team will need, how they will get it, and how they will remain on track in order to *avoid* having these elephants resurface. How will you be kept in the feedback loops you need to have? If elephants had been hiding in the dark, under the rug, what information flow has to be put in place so they don't return? This piece is important also to setting up the process that the team or organization will use to regularly go elephant-hunting. (See Chapter 13 for examples.)

Deep Learning & Potential: The leader and the group want to thrive. No one wants to be pulled down by hidden elephants and unresolved tensions and conflict; no organization wants to be less than it can be. So here is the opportunity to ask this very important question: What is the very best we could be, together, and in our work accomplishments, if we had no hidden, lurking elephants (if we always had a way to be addressing them)? If we do all the things we've committed to do in this process today, what is the best we could become? The best team ever? The best at what we do? The most effective? The most productive? The most profitable? The example for the company? What is that potential? Find that potential and embrace it—take it in. That becomes your new, overarching intention! With this new, deep learning, we can become exceptional.

Structure & Context:

Structure implies an internal look. This is important for the leader and the team to know. How are we connected? What is our hierarchy? What makes a team? What would make us a better team, structurally? How are we connected to the pieces of the larger organization? Are we networking across-the-board? How do we do that?

Are we isolated? How do we touch information nodes we need to have? How do we make our structure work to help us be the best we can be together?

Context implies an external look. With what other teams, organizations, companies, entities are we competing? Are we competing for resources, for position, for dollars, for status, for success in the marketplace? It is important to know that we are not protected islands. We are in an organization, or in a business, or in academia to achieve certain goals. Who is our competition and how well are they achieving their goals? How do we compare? It is important to ask ourselves how what we've done together today, in this elephant examination, will help us become more competitive.

We all need to know how we stack up regarding our competitive world—therein is an impetus for change—to survive, to succeed, to be the best we can be.

Congratulations! You've now completed the circle (the peripheral); it is time to do the second-round focus regarding Principles & Standards/Intentions, followed by the third round involving Principles & Standards, Potential/Deep Learning, and New Work. You've then completed an integral, interconnected circle of interrogating reality, finding your elephants, resolving your conflicts, and being honest about your commitments, and you're ready to move forward!

As you know, nothing is static in the business, organizational, or academic world; the world keeps turning. That's why what you've put in place to lift up and address your future elephants is so important. Congratulations again!

Can you do this? Yes! You can. Will it take a long time? No! This process is quick. While it may seem complicated, it is not, especially if you have a skilled facilitator—who is willing to dig deeply and truly interrogate reality—helping you! All you need is a place to create your large map (usually 6 sheets of easel paper taped together, and some colored markers). Lifting up the elephants and getting them addressed for the long-term can happen in 1 to 2 days of deep, honest exploration. Depending on the commitment and the size of the team, it could be completed in 4 to 6 hours. The ultimate gut-connecting question is this: are you and your team/group/organization/business ready and committed to "be real" and to put in place what is necessary to make sure the elephant-finding-and-addressing process remains evergreen? That you will continue to address the elephants you find hiding and lurking in your organization or team? *That is what matters most.*

   Can You See Them Now? (Elephants in our midst.)

Claire Knowles

Contact Claire Knowles:
716-622-7753
E-mail: Claire@CanYouSeeMeNow.com
        or CEFK1@aol.com
www.CanYouSeeMeNow.com

Postscript: Comedian Jimmy Durante is credited with one of the early popularizations of the *invisible elephant.* In 1935 he starred in a Broadway musical, *Jumbo,* by Billy Rose. In the famous scene, a police officer stopped him while he was leading a live elephant and asked him, "What are you doing with that elephant?" Jimmy Durante's reply was: "What elephant?" That response was a regular show-stopper.

Let's not allow your elephants to become show-stoppers!

References

Center for Self-Organizing Leadership, established 2002. Connecting Leaders, Learning, and Experience. www.CenterforSelfOrganizingLeadership.com. [Teaching leaders how to lead; understanding complexity in organizations; providing certification in Process Enneagram© facilitation.]

Dalmau, Tim (The Dalmau Group). *An Enclave of Enneagrams.* www.InquiryLearningChange.com/wp-content/uploads/2012/08/An_enclave_of_enneagrams_February_2006-copy.pdf. [Example Process Enneagram© templates.]

Elephant Idioms. www.en.Wikipedia.org/wiki/Elephant_in_the_room. [Includes early-origin reference to Jimmy Durante, 1935, Billy Rose stage musical, *Jumbo.*]

Knowles, Claire. 2012. *Lights On! A Reflective Journey…Illuminations to Move Your Life Forward With Ease.* Available on Amazon and Kindle.

Knowles, Richard. 2002. *The Leadership Dance…Pathways to Extraordinary Organizational Effectiveness.* Available on Amazon. [Complexity/Self-Organizing Leadership; The Process Enneagram©…the Map that Never Fails.]

McCarter, Beverly G, & White, Brian E. 2013. *Leadership in Chaordic Organizations.* CRC Press, Taylor & Francis Group. Available on Amazon.[Complex Adaptive Systems/Organizational Group Dynamics.]

O'Grady, Dr. Dennis. "The Elephant in the Room Stinks." New Insights Communications. Tools2Use/Talk2Me/Blog. www.DrOGrady.com/231/the-elephant-in-the-roomstinks/.

Scott, Susan. 2002, 2004. *Fierce Conversations … Achieving Success at Work & In Life, One Conversation at a Time*. Berkley Publishing Group, Division of Penguin Group USA. Available in fine bookstores, Amazon, and Kindle.

Stillman, Jessica. March 5, 2011. CBS News. MoneyWatch. www.CBSNews.com/8301-505125_162-38944297/be-less-self-centered-to-be-more-creative-study-says/. [References findings from two business school professors, Evan Polman at NYU and Kyle Emich at Cornell.]

Stoelting, Christine. 2012. *Color Me Perfect*. iTune App for iPhone, iPad, Lifestyles.iTunes.apple.com/us/app/color-me-perfect/id533849973?mt=8.

Praise for the Book

"For as long as I have known her, Claire Knowles has been hunting elephants. With a twinkle in her eye, keen intuition, and sophisticated tact, Claire identifies and broaches the dangerous territory of "undiscussables" in organizations with courage that is fueled by deep personal integrity and good old-fashioned common sense.

This book is a valuable eye-opener, written in her classic style, blending humor with no nonsense straight talk that creates in us deep awareness of the kind of behaviors we may unconsciously keep tucked away under the rug. Just when you begin waking up—absorbing deep content that traverses metaphor and hard business speak—she packs a punch that will keep you wide-eyed, by providing solutions with dynamic tools that enable us to make the paradigm shift essential to creating healthy, thriving organizations. This book is a must-read for all who are willing to take a hard, honest look at themselves and their organizations, and who are determined to lead, change and grow."

Patricia Brown
President, Integrated Business Ventures, Inc.
www.IntegratedBV.com

"*Elephants in Our Midst* is all about transparency, honesty, integrity and the strength of will to do what is truly best for our organizations. Claire Knowles gives us permission to deal with the many 'elephants' that hide in our organizations, and coaches us with encouragement and important insight."

Amy Jo Lauber
President, Lauber Financial Planning
President, New York State Women, Buffalo-Niagara Chapter
Author of: *Living Inspired and Financially Empowered*
www.LauberFinancialPlanning.com

"Claire Knowles knows what working with groups of people in tough business situations is all about. This book is a creative take on dealing with the 'elephants' that get in the way of our being the best we can be. Both leaders and leaders-to-be can take away ideas for how to be aware of, address, and deal with the 'elephants' that can hinder an organization's success."

Cathi Brese Doebler
Owner, Brese Doebler Performance Consulting
Author of: *Ditch the Joneses, Discover Your Family*
www.DitchThe.com

"We've all experienced the negative person who disrupts the flow of our business. Too often they get away with it because people lack the **courage** and/or skills to challenge them. Thankfully, Claire Knowles has written a handbook that inspires you to take charge and to successfully deal with the real issues. Powerful lessons. Insightful advice."

Marilyn Segal
Life Purpose Coach
Author of: *The Heart Speaks…Creating Your Own Heaven on Earth*
www.marilynsegal.com

"This book was eye-opening for both my business and non-profit. I can see many elephants that are getting in the way and that must be addressed in order to grow each. Now I know how to do this in a business effective way. Claire Knowles' book should be a 'must read' for anyone in a leadership position."

Renee L. Cerullo
President, RLComputing
President, Ed Tech Foundation of WNY
Officer, New York State Women, Inc.
www.RLComputing.com

"I thoroughly enjoyed this book. I laughed aloud as I thought about various ways that author, Claire Knowles, has taught Leaders how to lead by adeptly using elephant-in-the-room language. Her way of using *elephant speak* to get Leaders' attention and to teach us how to be most effective in the midst of elephants, is priceless! This book presents the tenets of Leadership in ways that every Leader can benefit!"

Mary K. Nassoiy
Chief Operating Officer, Financial Institution, NY State

"This book should be *required-reading* for all Leaders in every Organization—Business Management 101. Powerful Insights... presented with a serious-yet-whimsical approach for Leaders to address one's pesky organizational elephants. Addressing these issues Claire Knowles so clearly defines, will lead to massive positive change in your organization or business."

Jody Smith, CPC
Integrity Business Solutions
www.SmithIBS.com

"Any Elephants in the Room? Leaders that struggle with organizational transformation, culture change or change management can most certainly learn from Claire Knowles' creative look at the 'organizational elephants' that hinder success. She has provided the roadmap to lift up, address, and vanquish the elephants. The book is written simply, yet powerfully. Claire Knowles shares the final roadmap—the 'how-to' of it all is hugely insightful."

Kathy Perry
Stepping Stones to Success
Co-Author with Deepak Chopra, Jack Canfield & Dr. Denis Waitley
www.kathyperry.com

"You mean you didn't bring home the White Elephant?" Those are the words my father used whenever my mother returned from one of her shopping trips; she never missed the White Elephant sale. When I inquired what that statement meant, he would say that she bought everything else at the White Elephant sale. That left me wondering-- *why not the White Elephant?"*

"There's another big elephant lurking here—yet who knows of what color? *Can You See Them Now?* is a must read—a creative look at the "organizational elephants" that block success. This book, like the elephant – is hugely insightful, powerful, and courageously steps in to show us how to be truly effective leaders—the kind of leaders that want to move their groups forward in the right direction with authenticity and clarity."

"They may not be White Elephants, but Claire Knowles shows us the roadmap to lift up, address, and vanquish the troublesome organizational Elephants that need to be addressed. This book is not just for leaders, it applies to everyone--there are Elephants everywhere!"

Dori Montini-Kotzin
President, Western New York Women
www.WNYWomen.com

"This book is a spot on mix of professionalism, understanding and leadership. It is creative in its presentation...directly focusing on Leaders and Leadership for responsibly finding and resolving organizational elephants. **You don't have any? Better look again.** This book will show you how.

Claire Knowles' how-to-coaching to lift up and address those elephants that plague our respective organizations is powerful--yet as she shows us, is easy to apply. Insightful, straight-forward advice for every leader, manager, boss and supervisor!"

Laura Ward
HR, Training & Leadership Development Professional
St. Petersburg FL

"Claire Knowles, as the best selling author of Lights *On! A Reflective Journey ...Illuminations to Move Your Life Forward with Ease,* took us through a journey initially to take responsibility for personal growth. Now, with this book, she takes us to that next step where personal responsibility meets the need to assertively address what happens in organizational dynamics. Powerful insights...presented with a serious yet humor-filled approach for Leaders to address one's organizational elephant herd. Her road-map that never fails shows us how to vanquish our elephants in the real world of work! Bravo!

Nydia Santiago, PhD
Health & Wellness Professional
St. Petersburg, FL

"Claire Knowles is a champion of transparency and integrity in the workplace. Her playful pachyderm theme takes on serious organizational challenges and offers practical solutions."

Jill Geisler
Author, Best-selling book, *Work Happy: What Great Bosses Know*
Senior Faculty/Leadership and Management, The Poynter Institute
http://whatgreatbossesknow.com

"I very much enjoyed this book and will make it *required reading* in our company. Too much time is spent and production lost in dancing around issues that need to be acknowledged and resolved. Claire Knowles' approach, using a whimsical manner, makes the subject easy to acknowledge and attack. Her program to take charge and inspire is right on target."

Dale E. Weidemiller
President, Neal Communities Land Development
Bradenton, FL

"Claire Knowles has written a delightful and eminently useful guide to help leaders conquer the costly elephants that are trumpeting all around us, sapping the effectiveness of our organizations. The insights, hard-hitting questions, and practical tips she provides equip leaders to face those elephants with courage and resolve."

Richard Hadden,
Co-author, *Contented Cows Still Give Better Milk*
http://ContentedCows.com

"Outstanding...there's no hidden elephant in this book! Claire Knowles has done a magnificent and effective job of defining and illuminating what the elephant is and what it takes to address it (or them). She has absolutely nailed the entire concept AND the damage an elephant can produce—if not addressed. I love the light–yet-candid style she has used to write the book including the "elephant speak" and "business speak" counterpoints. I know there are elephants everywhere and this book is sorely needed. **As a business and leadership development coach, I'm recommending this book to everyone I come into contact with... professionally and personally.**"

Barry Foster, CRC, RCC, CPBA
Author of *Overcoming Your Funk*
Senior Advisory Board Member, National Association
of Business Coaches
Founder, The Corporate Coaching Center
www.everyoneneedsacoach.com

"Any woman who's ever been in the ladies room at work knows what an organizational elephant is, and how difficult it is to rid the organization of them. This book is a must-read for any leader who wants to truly lead—with sustained effectiveness. Claire Knowles shows us how!"

~Gloria Feldt
Author of *No Excuses:*
9 Ways Women Can Change How We Think About Power
President of Take The Lead

Point of View:

Having spent my career in Human Resource Management and Labor Relations dealing with diverse people issues, it became very apparent to me that so many conflicts and grievances could have been resolved much more quickly and effectively if people would "talk to each other" at the time of the conflict, rather than letting things fester over time. Now, in my consulting, I've found that this same situation arises in many companies, organizations, and workplaces. The resolution remains the same. Lifting up the elephants, dissecting them, understanding all the perspectives, addressing them—finding a way through the mire.

My primary work now is in working with organizations, and this is my point of view: I know that when workplaces can't, don't, or won't resolve their entrenched elephants, that things turn dysfunctional, and then the cruelness of people emerges—overtly or covertly, consciously or unconsciously, deliberately or unintentionally. People retreat inward and then give less than their best. Effectiveness plummets. Bad behavior (unprofessionalism) often emerges too. My deep mission is to help organizations co-create their future and build effectiveness along with kindness and humanity for the workplace. I work with leaders in big ways, because I'm firmly committed to the fact that if you are a leader, you have to lead. If you are not leading, you need to step up and learn how to lead effectively. So turning the "Lights On!" for getting whole-group clarity, coherence, and cooperation in the workplace is what I do for organizations that want to move forward with gusto.

Claire Knowles

- Best-selling author of *Lights On! A Reflective Journey* (www.LightsOnBook.com)
- Speaker for women's conferences, networks, retreats, groups
- Consultant to organizations, teams, businesses
- Success workshops
- Leadership (www.LightsOnLeadershipSuccess4Women.com)

Yes, You Can
Lift Up The Hidden Elephants Lurking In Your Organization!

CPSIA information can be obtained at www.ICGtesting.com
Printed in the USA
LVOW01s1823210715

447056LV00024B/1248/P